AFTER THE BUZZ COMES THE BEE

LIFT-THE-FLAP ANIMAL SOUNDS

BY **Rachel Isadora** & **Robie Rogge**

ILLUSTRATED BY **Rachel Isadora**

HOLIDAY HOUSE • NEW YORK

After the buzzzzzzzzzzzz . . .

After the ribbit-ribbit . . .

After the oink-oink . . .

After the baa-baa-baa . . .

After the huff, puff, squeak . . .

After the arr-arr-arr . . .

And after the ♩ ♩ ♪ ♫ ♩

comes the sleep.

Zzzzzzzzzz.

For our light, Lucia Rose —R.I.

To Hannah Blue —R.R.

HOLIDAY HOUSE is registered in the U.S. Patent and Trademark Office.

Printed and bound in December 2021 at Toppan Leefung, DongGuan, China.

The artwork was created with pen, ink, and watercolor.

www.holidayhouse.com

First Edition

1 3 5 7 9 10 8 6 4 2

Library of Congress Cataloging-in-Publication Data is available

Names: Rogge, Robie, author. | Isadora, Rachel, illustrator.
Title: After the buzz comes the bee : lift-the-flap animal sounds / Robie Rogge, Rachel Isadora.
Description: First edition. | New York City : Holiday House, [2022]
Audience: Ages 2–5 | Audience: Grades K–1 | Summary: "Buzz! Ribbit! Oink! Quack! Lift the flap
to find the animals that are making all the noise!" — Provided by publisher.
Identifiers: LCCN 2021014833 | ISBN 9780823449200 (hardcover)
Subjects: LCSH: Animal sounds—Juvenile literature.
Classification: LCC QL765 .R64 2022 | DDC 591.59/4—dc23
LC record available at https://lccn.loc.gov/2021014833